LEARN ABOUT AUTHORS AND ILLUSTRATORS

LISA OWINGS

Lerner Publications Company • Minneapolis

For my parents, who taught me to follow my dreams
and who believed I could make them come true

Lerner Publications Company
A division of Lerner Publishing Group, Inc.
241 First Avenue North
Minneapolis, MN 55401 U.S.A.

Website address: www.lernerbooks.com

Library of Congress Cataloging-in-Publication Data

Owings, Lisa.
    Learn about authors and illustrators / by Lisa Owings.
      pages   cm. — (Library smarts)
    Includes index.
    ISBN 978–1–4677–1502–7
    ISBN 978–1–4677–1752–6 (eBook)
    1. Authorship—Juvenile literature. 2. Authors—Juvenile literature.
  3. Illustrators—Juvenile literature. 4. Books—Juvenile literature.
  5. Libraries—Juvenile literature. I. Title.
  PN153.O95 2014
  808.02—dc23   2012049759

Manufactured in the United States of America
1 – CG – 7/15/13

TABLE OF CONTENTS

Authors and Illustrators

What is one of the best things about books? Books have words. The words tell a story. But how did the words get into the book? Someone had to write those words. Someone had to tell that story. That person is the **author**. An author writes books.

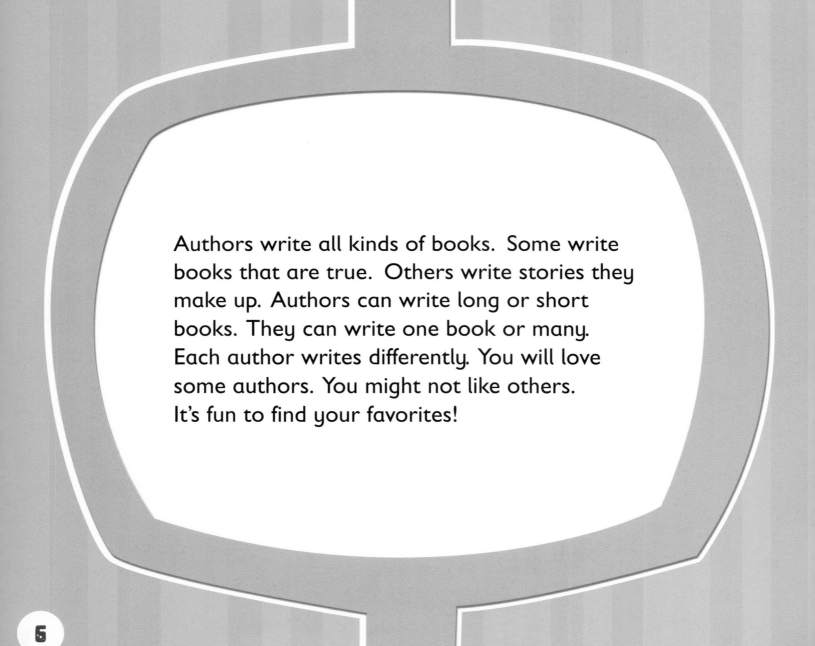

Authors write all kinds of books. Some write books that are true. Others write stories they make up. Authors can write long or short books. They can write one book or many. Each author writes differently. You will love some authors. You might not like others. It's fun to find your favorites!

What is another great thing about books? Lots of books have pictures. Pictures tell stories too. But how did the pictures get into the book? Someone had to make them. That person is the **illustrator**. An illustrator makes pictures to go in books.

Illustrators read an author's story. Then they make pictures to help tell the story. The pictures are called **illustrations**. The illustrations have to make sense with the story.

Some illustrators use pencils and pens. Others use paints. Still others use computers. What illustrations do you like best?

Authors and illustrators work together.
They tell the same story in different ways.
The words help you understand the pictures.
The pictures help you understand the words.

Look and Learn

The library is full of good books. Each one has an author. It's easy to find out who wrote a book. Look on the front **cover**. You'll see the **title**. The author's name is there too. It's written in smaller letters. Sometimes it has the word *by* in front of it. Can you find it?

THE BEST DOGS EVER

IRISH WOLFHOUNDS ARE THE BEST!

Elaine Landau

Lerner

Picture books have illustrators. The illustrator's name is also on the cover. Some picture books have only one name. That person is the author and the illustrator!

You can find more than names on a book. Check the back of the book. Look for a **summary** of what the book is about. Ask a **librarian** to help you.

Front cover:

cloverleaf books™

Fall's Here!

Fall Weather

Cooler Temperatures

Martha E. H. Rustad

Illustrated by Amanda Enright

Spine:

cloverleaf books™

Fall Weather: Cooler Temperatures   RUSTAD   Millbrook

Back cover:

Brrr! It's starting to get chilly! Find out how weather changes during fall. See how people and animals get ready for cooler temperatures. Let's grab our coats and mittens!

cloverleaf books™

Some books have shiny stickers. That means the book won an **award**. Some stickers say *Newbery*. Newbery awards are for authors. Those books have wonderful stories. Other stickers say *Caldecott*. Caldecott awards are for illustrators. Those books have beautiful pictures.

Who Are Authors and Illustrators?

Authors are regular people. The best authors are great storytellers. They love to write. Illustrators are regular people too. The best ones love to make art. They make beautiful pictures for books.

Can you be an author or an illustrator? Do you love to write? Do you love to make art? Then the answer could be yes! The best authors and illustrators read a lot. They find words that tell the best stories. Or they find ways to make the best pictures. Write *your* story. Make *your* pictures. You might find your name on a book one day.

GLOSSARY

author: a person who writes books

award: a prize for work well done

cover: the outside part of a book. The cover shows the title, author, and illustrator of a book. It also protects the pages.

illustrations: pictures in a book

illustrator: a person who makes pictures to go in books

librarian: a person who works in a library

summary: an explanation of main points. On the backs of some books, you'll find a summary of what they are about.

title: the name of a book

INDEX

Photo acknowledgments: The images in this book are used with the permission of: © iStockphoto.com/Blend_Images, p. 5; © iStockphoto.com/Jacek Chabraszewski, p. 7; © Todd Strand/Independent Picture Service, pp. 9, 11, 15, 17, 19; © Yellow Dog Productions/Lifesize/Getty Images, p. 13; © Cora Reed/Shutterstock.com, p. 21; © iStockphoto.com/WILLSIE, p. 23.

Front cover: © Nicolas Hansen/The Agency Collection/Getty Images.

Main body text set in Gill Sans Infant Std Regular 18/22. Typeface provided by Monotype Typography.

JUN 13 2014

For River Valley PLD
555 Barrington Ave., Dundee, IL 60118
www.frvpld.info
Renew online or call 847-590-8706